T0146946

STRATEGY OF DECEPTION

First published as *Stratégie de la déception* by Editions Galilee 1999

This translation published by Verso 2000

This edition published by Verso 2007

1 3 5 7 9 10 8 6 4 2

Verso
UK: 6 Meard Street, London W1F 0EG
USA: 388 Atlantic Ave, Brooklyn, NY 11217
www.versobooks.com

Verso is the imprint of New Left Books

ISBN-13: 978-1-84467-578-4
ISBN-10: 1-84467-578-5

British Library Cataloguing in Publication Data
A catalogue record for this book is available from the British Library

Library of Congress Cataloging-in-Publication Data
A catalog record for this book is available from the Library of Congress

Printed in the United States

For Father Patrick Giros

The Atlantic Alliance is perhaps in the end more a bastard child of the Communists than a child born because we wanted it.

Paul-Henri Spaak,
Secretary-General of NATO

AUTHOR'S NOTE

The first three articles reprinted here were written between 19 April and 15 June 1999 during the Kosovo conflict. The first was published on 27 April in the *Frankfurter Allgemeine Zeitung*. The fourth was completed on 5 July.

Translator's Note

on the French title, *Stratégie de la déception*

It is always disappointing to report something lost in translation. In this case, the element lost is that of disappointment itself, for this is, of course, the everyday meaning of the French word 'la déception'. The term does, however, also have a more recondite military sense, the *déception* of missiles being the overall process of the deflection of such weapons from their course (this part is, technically, their *séduction*) and their redirection to some other – preferably harmless – target. Virilio uses the term to refer to this bundle of techniques of decoying, distraction and disinformation which make up a classically 'deceptive' strategy in the modern English sense. However, in his title he is alluding also, and more directly, to the (possibly intended) disappointment and disillusionment which remains after the massive Allied military efforts in the former Yugoslavia, where, were we nineteenth-century speakers of English, we might contend (*pace* Jamie Shea) that 'never was expectation more completely deceived'.[1]

1 James Mill, *The History of British India* (1817), vol. II, p. 89.

CHAPTER 1

'Reason deceives us more often than nature,' claimed Vauvenargues.[1] However that may be, the nature of the terrain in the Balkans seems to have been totally left out of account in the reasoning of NATO's war leaders. In allowing no tactical distance between their political goals and their chosen means of action, the strategists of the Atlantic Alliance have once again revealed the shakiness of their military conceptions and the fragility of those scenarios in which, since the end of the Cold War, the technical illusionism of the United States has found expression.

1 Luc de Clapiers Vauvenargues, French essayist and moralist, 1715–1747.

In a recent interview, Tony Blair declared: 'This is a new kind of war, about values as much as territory.'[2] In so saying, he indicated, if not that geopolitics had followed history in coming to an end, at least that the Allies have now ceased to attach importance to the physical conditions of a battle being fought against a well-entrenched adversary in an environment which is both *geologically* and *geopolitically* tormented.

General Wesley Clark, an enthusiastic supporter of warfare remote-controlled by satellite from space, pointed out on 13 April 1999 in Brussels: 'This campaign has the highest proportion of precision weaponry that has ever been used in any air operation anywhere.'[3] This massive use of high technology, though purportedly employed to avoid causing 'collateral' damage, would not prevent the Commander-in-Chief apologizing shortly afterwards for a number of 'regrettable incidents', such as the bombing of refugee columns.

In fact, by vaunting the technical supremacy of aerial devices in this way, General Clark was not so much setting himself up as the spokesman for NATO power as for the theorists of the Pentagon's 'revolution in military affairs' (RMA). Those theorists have for some years now

2 P. Stephens, 'Fighting a Just War', *Financial Times*, 16 April 1999.

3 NATO briefing, 13 April 1999.

been minded to extend *automatic missile strikes* indefinitely: over deserts (Operation Desert Fox in Iraq) and across countries over-flown with impunity (anti-terrorist operations in Sudan and Afghanistan), as though the aim were henceforth to extend the Open City concept of past territorial conflicts to the air-space of sovereign nations, with the 'open sky' of **tele-war** now strategically complementing the economic deregulation of air transport, which was given that selfsame code name: Open Sky.

Whereas the systematic use of those new 'ships of the desert', the 'Cruise Missiles', 'Drones' and other unidentified flying devices such as the F 117, was possible in the desert conditions of the Gulf War, the mountainous territory of the Balkans meant there was no hope of a 'lightning campaign' and NATO was going to be dragged down a military cul-de-sac – the lack of geopolitical foresight in Operation **Allied Force** being well illustrated by the soliciting of Russian involvement.

As early as 1997, the Pentagon's Quadrennial Defense Review looked forward to the USA having a capability to carry on *two major wars* at the same time, while simultaneously fulfilling several *emergency missions* of a limited character to 'restore peace' in various unimportant parts of the world. Two years later, we have to conclude, if not that that programme has failed, then at least that there is a danger of a symbolic and media defeat more serious than the one suffered in Somalia, and also that a new arms race in (atomic, chemical . . .) weapons of mass destruction has begun in many countries which have concerns for their national sovereignty.

In this sense, the new ground broken with the allegedly *humanitarian war* for Kosovo could not but trouble a growing number of 'weak' nations, and confirm the views of all those who fear some day becoming targets of the 'strong' ones.

If this were in fact the case, the *counter-productive* character of the air strikes which were supposed to prevent a humanitarian catastrophe befalling the Kosovo refugees (a tragedy those strikes singularly accelerated) would be further reinforced by the (in this case *very long-term*) counter-productivity of the re-launch, not of a Cold War with opportune deterrence, but of a growing threat of nuclear, chemical and bacteriological proliferation in countries concerned to forearm themselves on a long-term basis against the effects of an attack involving weapons of mass destruction and yet not able to employ high-precision weapons remotely guided from space. In this connection the reaction of India is particularly revealing:

> The nations which wish to preserve their strategic autonomy and their political sovereignty have no other option than to maintain their nuclear arsenals, develop missiles and attempt to

> improve their military capabilities. The latter aim being long-term and expensive, the cheapest way in the meantime – before strategic parity is achieved – is to concentrate on missile development. *It is to anticipate this logic that the United States decided to develop an anti-missile defence and to prevent the acquisition of those technologies by other countries.*[4]

This particularly fearsome view of the future is shared by Russia and Ukraine – and also by Japan, which has just launched an observation satellite to protect itself against the missiles of a currently disintegrating North Korean state.

So far as the conflict in Kosovo is concerned, then, *whatever the outcome of that conflict*, the question arises – a question masked since the pseudo-victory in the Gulf War – of *an unbalance of terror* in which the infinite spread of weapons of mass destruction would no longer leave any room for *inter-state deterrence.*

In the history of nations the development of armies, navies, air forces – and now space forces – has in each case prompted developments in armaments and political

4 *The Times of India*, 2 April 1999.

strategies. If we want to analyse the failure of NATO today (its failure, we may repeat, whatever the outcome of the war in Kosovo), we have to look back over the origins of air supremacy, which followed upon centuries when command of the seas was paramount.

The theory of *air power*, first propounded by the Italian Giulio Douhet, was an attempt to build on the theory of *sea power*. The idea of winning a war from up in the sky – that Marinettian, Futurist vision – was soon taken over by the founder of the Royal Flying Corps, General Trenchard, who tried out the use of massive air raids on rebel tribes in Britain's Near Eastern colonies. Later an American, General Billy Mitchell, had the idea of combining air and naval forces, becoming the advocate of the aircraft carrier. In spite of the Luftwaffe's offensives, the 'Blitz' and the strategic bombing of Germany in the Second World War, Douhet's theory that air forces could win a war without support from land forces was not to receive confirmation until Hiroshima, when *a single B 29 bomber and a single atom bomb put an end to the war in the Pacific.*[5]

During the Cold War years, the development of 'intercontinental missiles' and control of satellite space

5 Some political analysts took the view that the Nagasaki bomb was unnecessary.

for the guidance of high-precision missiles sadly caused us to forget the fact that aero-spatial war goes hand in hand with extremes of destruction and *the imperative need for an absolute weapon*, whether it be an atomic or neutron device, or chemical/bacteriological agents. It was because this fact was forgotten, or rather obscured by the illusion of Allied victory in Iraq, that the fatal error was to arise during the Clinton presidency of an all-out multiplication of these 'automatic strikes', aimed at punishing so-called 'rogue states', from which the USA aspires to protect the world by way of its telematic technologies.

And indeed, going beyond the 'humanitarian' basis of the Kosovo conflict, the Pentagon spokesman Kenneth Bacon was to declare on 16 April 1999: 'We believe there is still a chemical weapons capability of unknown quantity in Yugoslavia today.' That declaration, a prelude to an imminent change of course in the Balkans, well illustrated the limits of the famous *duty to intervene*. This is not an *ethical* limit, as one might naïvely believe, but a *strategic* limit, such as the limit which, in the case of *nuclear deterrence* more than forty years ago, imposed the *terroristic equilibrium between East and West* – but did so at the cost of putting all life on the planet under threat of extinction. This was a genuine *crime against humanity*, though no penal sanction will ever be taken against it!

Thus, after the momentous political repudiation of the United Nations and, in the near future perhaps, the repudiation of NATO's power of *defensive* control, we would seem to be embarking upon another kind of control – in this case, *offensive* – in which the **military** no longer pretends to 'play cops and robbers' with murderous rogue states, but regains its old place in the face of the difficulties of the **politicians** to manage the **new world order** effectively. When you see the nature of the decisions taken by the military general staff of NATO, in which the nineteen capitals of the Alliance have to give the same 'mission order' in what the generals refer to as a **silence procedure** – a process whereby they *give the green light by implicit consensus* – you can see how limited are the prospects for this form of 'politics continued by other means'. The need to arrive at a consensus of NATO member states on every tactical operation and target can only produce losses of precious time for action on the ground, seriously prejudicing that *speed which is the essence of war.*

But let us come back to this question of *universal values* which should, according to Tony Blair, begin to supplant the question of *territories* and the sovereignty of nation states. When you claim to prosecute a war in the name of 'human rights' – a humanitarian war – you deprive yourself of the possibility of negotiating a cessation of hostilities with your enemy. If the enemy is a torturer, *the enemy of the human race*, there is no alternative but the extremes of *total war* and unconditional surrender. We can see, then, that this new logic of war leads, like the aero-spatial strategy which underpins it, to the uncontrolled 'escalation' condemned by theorists of international geopolitics.

Let us remember, for example, Yitzhak Rabin's riposte to General Sharon, when the latter harangued him in the Knesset after the Camp David Accords. 'You negotiated with the terrorist Arafat, which is shameful!' taunted the general. To gales of laughter from the Israeli parliament Rabin retorted: 'But, my friend, to make peace you have to negotiate with the enemy!' The introduction of the superiority of 'universal values' over political territory goes together, then, with a stealthy, discreet invention (in this respect it is similar to many of the craft involved in the Allied air offensive): the invention of a **secular holy war**, for which the fundamentalism of the 'duty to intervene' might be said to lay the ground. Behind this sudden deterritorialization of a conflict which President Clinton still refuses to call a **war** lies, then, the *tragi-comic infantilization* of this century's end, when the impeachment procedure against the American president is still present in all our memories.

Discipline being the major force of armies, there cannot in fact be 'genuine war' without a *war leader.* It remains, then, for us to inquire how much decision-making power Bill Clinton possesses after the disastrous impact of 'Monicagate'. Behind the attacks directed at

Madeleine Albright, whose influence is fading, it is clearly the American president who is the target, to such an extent indeed that we may wonder whether Clinton has not already been discreetly removed from office . . . We may recall that, after his public confession on the world's TV screens, Bill Clinton had called the military leaders of the Pentagon to the White House and reaffirmed that he remained leader of the armed forces. Furthermore, legal proceedings were begun by the presidency against military personnel who had mocked him.

If Yeltsin is not Gorbachev, the former KGB man, neither is Clinton Bush, the former CIA agent. As for the return of Primakov, this event confirmed that, in a period of information war, the intelligence services of the military men have come back to compensate for the congenital weaknesses and infantilism of the politicians.

'What difference is there between an adult and a child?' a Las Vegas hotel-owner was asked. Answer: '*The price of his toys*!' With the doctrine of the 'revolution in military affairs', American technology seems to be becoming today, for Bill Clinton, a sort of **Wonderland** in which the warrior, like a child in its playpen, wants to *try out everything, show off everything*, for fear of otherwise seeming weak and isolated. In Kosovo, as not so long ago in Iraq, the last great power has both to engage in a sympathy *offensive* (the term is apposite) and establish its global hegemony by exhibiting its arsenal of weapons, including Cruise Missiles and F 117s, already used in

Iraq, and the B2 bombers, each of which has a unit cost equal to the GNP of a country like Albania. And another illustration of this infantilization is provided by Bill Gates who in a recent book, among other things, extols the positive role played by the 'Falcon View' software in destroying bridges in the Balkans.[6]

Scorning 'nature' in the name of 'computer reason', *fin-de-siècle* America (unlike the America which contributed to the salvation of the free world) is transplanting its *systemic rationality* into programmed automata, into 'smart' missiles, as though the world were a toy or a war game and Bill Gates its prophet; a prophet who in 1998 did not hesitate to lecture Bill Clinton himself on the importance of a power which is perhaps no longer the power of the *political sphere* and the elected statesman, but rather that of the computer engineer, the programmer – for whom Gates, in spite of his trial, remains the model.

And America is transplanting that systemic rationality even into the sphere of the conquest of space, where space probes – those other 'cruise missiles' – (such as Deep Space 1) are supplanting the astronauts of NASA's manned flights, in the same way as automatic devices are replacing the official commitment of US forces.

---

6 Bill Gates, *Business @ the Speed of Thought: Using a Digital Nervous System*, Warner Books, New York, 1999.

On 5 May 1999, six weeks after air operations in the Balkans began, Senator Lucien Neuvirth, who chairs the French Parliamentary Committee on Space, wrote:

> Satellite observation and multimedia development are expressions of a historic change. *Technological development is increasingly putting society at the heart of space affairs*. Possessing means of observation and action, having a choice of response, *being less predictable* – these are so many characteristics which define a power. Keeping the space sector, like defence, outside the European Union, shows that governments have not yet manifested a strong desire to integrate *this other sector of sovereignty*.[7]

With its calls for independent access to, and navigation in, space, and independence in the observation of the earth, *space law* takes over almost word for word the old language of *maritime law*. After the 1930s myth of the 'flying nation', which heralded the development of the air power that was soon to lay Europe waste from Rotterdam to Dresden and from Coventry to Hamburg, we are seeing today, with the war in Kosovo, the

7 *Le Figaro*, 5 May 1999.

emergence of the myth of the 'weightless' nation, *the floating nation.*[8]

The space sector, which is vital to the European states in the face of competition from the USA, is gradually coming to be the guarantee of a continent's security. So much so, indeed, that we may now, with regard to national sovereignty, ask the eccentric question *par excellence: is orbital space destined in the future to supplant territorial space?* If this were indeed the case, strategy would become not so much a matter of geography as of ecology, and the aureole which can be seen only from extra-atmospheric space, the 'light glow' produced by the ring of oxygen which encircles the earth and makes it habitable, would have become the last *stage* [*scène*] of history.

With *air* and *space* law henceforth taking precedence over the law on the ownership and use of habitable *lands*, this slim atmospheric layer would then emerge as an arena of political conflict to succeed the devastating myth of **Lebensraum**. To lead the nations of the twenty-first century, it would no longer be a question so much of observing what is happening *on those countries' frontiers*, as what is happening *above* them, towards the

8 On the 'flying nation', see F. Thiede and E. Schmae, *Die fliegende Nation*, Union Deutscher Verlag, Berlin, 1933, especially pp. 140–41.

firmament, and this would be no small matter, since this 'lofty, extraterrestrial vantage point' would cancel out any geopolitical perspective, the *vertical* dimension winning out by a very long way – or, more exactly, from a very great height – over the *horizontal*.

The untimely air offensive on the Balkans, which exceeds the legitimate authority of the UN in terms of international security, can be seen, then, to mark a deep transformation in more ways than one in the nature of conflicts between nations. Gradually becoming an unhealthy climate, *a noxious atmosphere*, not so much by the emission of poison gases as by the unleashing of repeated magnetic storms, total war is now directed not so much against the enemy's war machines as against the *atmospheric ecosystem* of the target country. Hence the strange inversion in the nature of the victims of a conflict unleashed 'in the name of human rights' – a conflict in which most of the casualties are civilians and the military personnel appear to be a protected species.

Atmosphere, atmosphere . . .[9] Only yesterday, combatants were content merely to deceive the enemy, to disturb the limited electronic environment of his

9 'Atmosphère, atmosphère . . .': one of the most famous lines in French film history, delivered by Arletty in Marcel Carné's *Hôtel du Nord*.

weapons systems by jamming the airwaves. In the not too distant future, the great disturbance will be effected on the scale of a whole nation's meteorology.

The war with *zero deaths* for the military, but also *zero victories* in political terms, such as we are seeing in Kosovo, will give way to a **weapons ecosystem** capable of setting off the chain reaction of a *full-scale cybernetic accident*, in which disruption of the airwaves will predominate over the ravages caused by bombing. Further reinforcing the disorder and chaos occasioned by viruses and other 'logic bombs', the pollution of magnetic fields[10] will render wholly unpredictable the episodes of a conflict which will have itself become **surrealistic**!

---

10 *Les Champs magnétiques* is the title of a work by the Surrealists André Breton and Philippe Soupault. [Trans.]

CHAPTER 2

> Victory above all will be
> To see clearly at a distance
> To see everything
> Near at hand
> And may all things bear a new name,

wrote Guillaume Apollinaire in a war poem.[11] That new name today is **global information dominance**. In 1997, General Fogelman, Chief of Staff of the US Air Force, told the House of Representatives: 'In the first

11 Apollinaire, 'Victoire', *Caligrammes*. Trans. Anne Hyde Greet, University of California Press, Berkeley/London, 1980, p. 341.

three months of the twenty-first century, we shall be capable of finding, tracking and targeting virtually in real time any significant element moving on the surface of the earth.'[12] Confirming the validity of this Cyclopean vision, Rear-Admiral Brown, an officer of US Space Command, recently exclaimed in a press conference on Kosovo that US capacity to communicate using satellites had become 'simply phenomenal!'

We may conclude, then, that after the 'electronic warfare' deployed against Iraq, the United States has now launched 'information warfare'. And the power of this system rests on three fundamental principles: *the permanent presence of satellites* over territories, the *real-time transmission* of the information gathered and, lastly, the *ability to perform rapid analysis* of the data transmitted to the various general staffs.

There are currently some fifty satellites of all types and some twenty different space systems above the Balkans: these include National Reconnaissance Office (NRO) radar imagers, optical imagers belonging to the various branches of the services, not to mention the satellites listening in to electromagnetic signals which identify the movement of forces on the ground and,

---

12 Cited by F. Filloux, 'Le Pentagone la tête dans les étoiles', *Libération*, 20 April 1999.

also, of course, the constellation of satellites which make up the **global positioning system** (GPS), which pass on their positions to the vehicles and devices in action. Lastly, at high altitude, flying at 15,000 feet to avoid Serb anti-aircraft defences, there are the craft of manned air reconnaissance. And, flying lower, the automatic reconnaissance 'drones'.

Without this truly **panoptical** vision, the conflict in the Balkans would be condemned to repeat the strategies of yesteryear: *cordoning off* the battlefield, hemming the enemy in with *barrage fire* from the artillery or *strafing* by fighter-bombers. Let us note, however, that the Serb forces have countered this capability for total monitoring of *any significant element moving on the surface of the earth* by scattering and remaining static – that is to say, by apparent inertia – as they await a frontal assault which the Allies seem unable to resolve to undertake. Hence the patent failure of the NATO air strategy and the repeatedly deferred decision to mount a blockade of Yugoslavia.

Moreover, it is interesting to see how normal procedure has been reversed in this 'phoney war' in the Balkans. In the past, before you attacked a citadel, you camped around its ramparts and laid siege to it. In this case, since the spring of 1999, movement on the ground has been only partially interdicted; on the other hand, bomb upon bomb and missile after missile rained down before a debate on the possibility of a naval blockade began on 24 April. Yet, by contrast with the Kuwaiti desert, Yugoslavia is a *geological fortress* with mountainous terrain and, from the days of nationalist resistance against the Nazis to the organization by Tito of his famous popular defence system which was to enable the Yugoslav model of self-determination to withstand the might of the Soviets, it has been shown to possess many traps for the unwary.

But we have to go back to the Allied air offensive on Europe between 1943 and 1945 to understand the fatal error in 'Operation Allied Force'. In that period, Hitler's army and its Axis partners had managed to transform the continent of occupied Europe into a real *fortress*, ringing its coasts and frontiers with numerous, multi-layered lines of defence, including the famous 'Atlantic Wall'. Yet, as British Air Chief Marshal Arthur Harris pointed out, *Fortress Europe is 'a fortress without a roof, since we have air supremacy'*.

Almost sixty years later, the situation has been curiously reversed: the Balkans is a *natural fortress*, but a fortress without walls, where no state of siege exists to lock in the defenders and literally throttle their supply lines before the final assault. General Kelche, chief of the French general staff, explained: 'We're going to put a lid on Yugoslavia.' As though the Allies' air supremacy made it possible for them to stifle the enemy without any 'saucepan' for him to 'stew' in! This is a strange military logic in which the chaos of the war directives seems only to highlight the political chaos of this 'Balkan powder keg', where conflict, free-booting and smugglers' rings are second nature, ancient custom . . . to say nothing of the religious dimension of this former march of the Ottoman Empire.

But the other aspect of the **information war** today concerns the 'humanitarian' dimension of this very first 'human rights conflict' – a conflict in which civilian populations are in the front line. By way of confirming this paradox, let us take a look at some **panoptical** events which preceded the air attack on the offices of RTS, the Yugoslavian television station in Belgrade.

On 12 April, the ABC channel informed its viewers that the Pentagon had in its possession satellite images which proved the existence of mass graves in Kosovo. The channel referred to 'around a hundred places where the earth had been dug over', but ABC did not show a single one of these pictures, when in fact the decimetric high-definition of military photographs is of such precision that the likelihood of this kind of *proof by image* being achieved is very great. Moreover, two days earlier, the Pentagon had shown satellite photographs of groups of Kosovars camping out in the hills after fleeing their villages. ABC did not, however, specify the possible correlation between this exodus of unfortunates and the possibility of their having been massacred.

After the eye of God pursuing Cain into the tomb, we now have the *eye of Humanity* skimming over the oceans and continents in search of criminals. One gets an idea, then, of the *ethical* dimension of the **global information dominance** programme, the attributes of which are indeed those of the *divine*, opening up the possibility of *ethical cleansings,* which now seem set fair to replace the *ethnic cleansing* of undesirable or supernumerary populations. After denunciation by word of mouth, rumour, agents of influence and traditional spying, comes the age of *optical snooping*: this 'real time' of a **panoptical** large-scale optics, capable of monitoring not just *enemy*, but also friendly, movements thanks to the control of public opinion.

In fact the *television* of yesteryear here becomes purely and simply **global tele-surveillance** of social or asocial behaviour, of those 'attitudes' which advertising has worked for decades now to engineer. Above and beyond the widely remarked birth, ten years ago, of the **CNN–Pentagon pool**, large-scale satellite optics officially heralds the over-exposure of the nations to the 'gaze of the All-High', that **Cyclops** untroubled by any scruple.

All this enables us to explain the innovative, symbolic importance of the bombing of the offices of Belgrade television, which was a prelude not, as in the Persian Gulf, to a *war of images*, but to *the policing of images*, to the organization of a single market of global imagery, which found its confirmation in the creation of NIMA. In late 1996, the National Imagery and

Mapping Agency was born.[13] With 10,000 employees in its offices at Fairfax, Virginia, this agency, which was initially intended to process and distribute space images for the Pentagon and the CIA, was to engage two years later in *the monitoring of flows of commercial imagery* in order to become the obligatory conduit for civilian images, the need for which continues to rise with the globalization of trade. After the 'big ears' of the National Security Agency's 'Echelon' network, which have enabled Allied communications to be intercepted over the last ten years, the National Imagery and Mapping Agency has at last opened its 'big eyes'.

Following on from the deregulation of air transport in the early 1990s, on the eve of the year 2000 we saw the sudden deregulation of *space imagery transmissions*. The '*Open Sky*' strategy is not content, then, merely to continue the *Open City* strategy of the dim and distant days when nations enjoyed territorial sovereignty: it is extending its matchless transparency to the atmospheric scale of the planetary ecosystem.

---

13 NIMA was formed in October 1996 by consolidating the Defense Mapping Agency, the Central Imagery Office, the Defense Dissemination Program Office, the National Photographic Interpretation Center and the imagery exploitation and dissemination elements of the Defense Intelligence Agency, the National Reconnaissance Office, the Defense Airborne Reconnaissance Office and the Central Intelligence Agency. [Trans.]

The logistics of perception **on all fronts** has won out over the logistics of weapons targeted along a particular front, or rather along that *absence of front* characterizing this *absence of declared war,* where everything takes place only on screens. On 23 April 1999, by bombing the Serbian television building in Belgrade for the first time, NATO inaugurated a *nodal war*, which is merely the obverse of the *total war* of the mid-twentieth century.

Even if the European consortium which manages the TV-EUTELSAT satellite, whose leading members are Great Britain, Italy, France and Germany – and also the former Yugoslavia represented by Republic of Serbia – hesitated for a considerable time before *cutting off that satellite's feeds to Yugoslav television*, it did nonetheless resolve to do so at the end of May 1999, thus creating a troubling precedent where 'non-discrimination' in respect of community information is concerned. That act, combined with the pure and simple destruction of the main Serb media, is an illustration here and now of the conflict that is looming between *air* supremacy and *space* supremacy in a war of the airwaves.

In the era of **infowar**, when the cybernetics of systems tends to dominate the life of nations in the economic and political fields – and particularly in the field of global geopolitics – the innovation of controlling an enemy's information flows in this way far exceeds the mere jamming of his broadcasts, since it tends to suppress all telecommunications between the enemy state and its own population, and to do so whatever the nature of the message transmitted – active propaganda or passive information essential to the survival of the civilian populations.

There is a great deal to say about this 'control' of information flows, this totalitarian form of *media intervention* in which bombs replace the arguments and counter-propaganda directed at battered communities. This was, indeed, very clearly explained to the *New York Times* by Svetlana Radosevic, a sports commentator on RTS Belgrade when she said: '*If you think I'm lying, you don't need to kill me to prove it!*'[14]

But here again, the air supremacism of the Balkan conflict perfectly illustrates the difference in the images depending on the particular media concerned. All the reporters and eye-witnesses agree that now: '*Only the chaos on the ground enables you to escape propaganda.*'[15] And, just as the chaos of the geological formation of the Balkans is a serious *military* handicap for NATO, so the confusion and chaos of information is a *political* handicap in attempting to assess the war aims of this military coalition.

To illustrate these remarks on the 'war of the

---

14 Steven Erlanger, 'Survivors of NATO attack on Serb TV Headquarters . . .', *New York Times*, 24 April 1999.

15 M. Guérin, 'Objectifs de guerre', *Le Monde*, 2 May 1999.

airwaves' over Serbia, let us now observe the change in the Allied objective which came with the question, if not of how to implement a 'state of siege', at least of how to bring about the maritime isolation of this precipitously hilly region.

For want of a **naval blockade** of the Adriatic coast, which would be difficult, and which, in the absence of UN resolutions to that effect, France and Germany wanted to avoid, the Pentagon decided to deprive Yugoslavia of electricity by dropping graphite bombs capable of plunging it into large-scale black-out on its cities. Defence spokesperson Kenneth Bacon explained this new strategy in the following terms: 'It does confuse their command and control system; . . . it disorientates and confuses their computers.'[16]

During the Gulf War, as soon as the alarm sounded, the lights went out in Baghdad as a form of *passive defence.* With the conflict in Kosovo, we have a *passive offensive,* with the attackers themselves producing the interruption of Belgrade's electricity supply. When you know the strategic importance of this primary energy source in these days of 'information revolution', you are better placed to understand the logic of this act of war interrupting all

16 The text here is taken directly from the official transcript of the US Department of Defense's news briefing of 2.00 p.m., Monday, 3 May 1999. [Trans.]

communications. After the *media intervention* against the enemy's audio-visual resources, we suddenly have energy intervention – an intervention which casts into a totally new light the question of the economic blockade of the country. Jamie Shea, star presenter of Operation Allied Force, was later to declare in Brussels that NATO now had its finger on the off-switch in Yugoslavia.

In fact the BLU 114 B bomb used in the offensive against power generation in Serbia is a 'soft' bomb only in appearance, and by virtue of its low payload. Used on a power station in a high-voltage environment saturated with static electricity and ozone, graphite would act like an electric arc. This would quickly produce a serious fire and a terrible detonation.[17] When you know that, in a nuclear war, atomic power stations are major targets, you can better understand the value of the test carried out by NATO in the Balkans.

The subjects and solutions proposed by NATO and its Committee on the Challenges of Modern Society for consideration by its experts at the conference which met in Autumn 1973, are

17 B. Bombeau, 'BLU, la bombe au graphite: une arme potentiellement redoutable', *Air et Cosmos*, 7 May 1999.

> significant – in particular the pilot project for '*the universal planning of the circulation of persons and goods*'. These kinds of study are no longer concerned with somewhat distant visions of economic planning of the Hague Conference type. Though notions of this kind remain the purported motive and are still provisionally the means employed, they no longer define the event, *which now consists in putting in question, in the shorter or longer term, all human movement on the planet through the global strategic web spun by the new military–industrial complex.*[18]

When I penned these lines at the height of the Cold War a quarter of a century ago, I did not expect to find them becoming fiercely topical again in the days of the great post-industrial migration of this millennium end – on the one hand, with the exodus of the Kosovo refugees and, on the other, with immigration into western Europe from the eastern states or the southern shores of the Mediterranean – not to speak of the exodus of millions of Africans from areas of endemic tribal warfare or the need, with globalization, for

18 P. Virilio, *L'insécurité du territoire*, Galilée, Paris, 1993, p. 74 (First edition: Stock, Paris, 1976).

companies to transfer jobs to countries with lower labour costs.

On 24 March 1999, the very day when air strikes on Yugoslavia began and the moment when the 'ethnic cleansing' of the Kosovars was about to be speeded up, *the OECD called on the European Union also to speed up the mobility of labour within our continent*: 'The number of EU nationals resident in another Member State is only 5.5 million out of 370 million, equivalent to 1.5% of the population,' observed the OECD authors. They pointed out that mobility was greater in the USA, Canada or Australia, as though it was all a parlour game or an Olympic marathon![19]

A few weeks after the OECD expressed this desire, a million Kosovars were cast into limbo, being either deportees, political refugees from Serbian aggression or social refugees from an unemployment which, for the purposes of facilitating macro-economic adjustments, has become structural. Here, Milosevic's *ethnic cleansing* ran alongside the *technical cleansing* of the post-industrial proletariat. Faced with such large-scale movements of population and depopulation, it is infinitely easier to understand the military-industrial importance of the systems for locating vehicles and devices on the surface

19 OECD, *EMU: Facts, Challenges and Policies*, Paris, 1999.

of the planet, such as the **global positioning system** – a system running parallel to, and complementing, the **global information dominance** which makes it possible for the air offensive in the Balkans to be conducted today.

But the general public was as yet unaware that during the night of 21–22 August 1999 – four months before the millennium (Y2K) bug – *that system, linked to a network of military satellites, would experience its first 'cyber-accident'*. On that night, *the counter on the GPS receivers installed in vehicles* – the capacity of which was mysteriously limited to 1,024 weeks – *would 'roll back' to zero*. This is not yet the 'great meltdown' of the year 2000, but a dress rehearsal for the users of (civil and military) vehicles equipped with this location device. Officially, it was to be announced in June that NATO's military personnel had already modified the equipment that was affected by this 'rollback', such as Cruise Missiles or the GPS-guided bombs dropped by the B2 bomber which were reportedly responsible for destroying the Chinese embassy in Belgrade.

Regarding this *war of the airwaves*, which is being carried on in the electromagnetic ether over the Balkans, let us now observe two complementary aspects which are often dissociated for the purposes of the NATO cause: on the one hand, the suspension, to which we have already referred, of the television feeds of the **EUTELSAT** satellite on 26 May 1999 in order to 'Shut down the Serb propaganda machine' and, on the other, the launch on the Allied side of the **Commando Solo** missions of the four-engined Hercules EC 130E, a plane bristling with directional aerials and carrying a radio and television station in its cargo hold. 'When they arrive in the combat zone, the on-board operators broadcast messages pre-recorded in Serbo-Croat developed by the psychological operations department at Fort Bragg, the famous "psy ops" of information warfare. They are aided by five specialists in electronic warfare, at least one of whom is a linguist who can cut into programmes. Commando Solo can then distribute its TV programmes over a medium-sized conurbation, while its radio broadcasts can be heard over an area spanning several hundred kilometres.'[20]

With this clash in Hertzian space, which is a continuation of the clash in the air-space of the Balkans, the prophecy of Soviet Admiral Sergei Gorchkov is coming true. Some twenty years ago he predicted that 'The winner of the next war will be the one who makes best use of the electromagnetic spectrum.' This *spectre*, to use the French term, is a spectre haunting not just Europe,

20 P. Brunet, 'La guerre de l'information au Kosovo', *Air et Cosmos*, 14 May 1999.

but the world – the **unipolar** world that has come out of the Cold War.

To remain within this Hertzian space for a moment – the medium for the signals issuing from air-space – let us also mention a very recent development in detection techniques: 'multi-static detection using non-co-operative broadcasts'. With this revolutionary concept, developed by the Soviets, radar becomes outdated, since television can substitute for the surveillance radar of air traffic control and 'detect aircraft in flight at any point in atmospheric space'.[21] This 'multi-static detection' is limited only by the range of TV broadcasting or relay stations.

If we take the example of Britain, since the BBC covers the whole of the territory, the whole of Britain bathes in the Hertzian ether of television. In this electromagnetic layer, audio-visual signals behave as would the signals emitted by continuous-wave radar. As soon as an aircraft in flight is struck by an electromagnetic signal, it bounces back part of that signal. To detect the aircraft one merely needs an ordinary TV set with two standard aerials and a system for processing and amplifying the signal received. It is this system, dubbed

21 S. Brosselin, 'Guerre des ondes: le RADAR squatte la télévision', *Le Monde de l'aviation*, 12 May 1999.

'Silent Sentry', which Lockheed-Martin decided to reveal to the public in autumn 1998.

The two main advantages of this 'Hertzian ecosystem' are, on the one hand, the indestructible character of the detectors, which cover the whole of the enemy territory, and, on the other, the unprecedented possibility of reconfiguring the strategic detection architecture and extending it world-wide. '*By establishing a database that included the 55,000 aerials of the TV channels and FM radio stations spread throughout the world, and by interconnecting them, it would be possible, with* **TV radar**, *to cover the whole of the airspace of the two hemispheres.*'[22] With this sudden amplification of detection 'on all fronts', public television is no longer merely a **panoptical** tele-surveillance: it becomes a cosmic phenomenon in which intervention through the airwaves detects any activity, any movement, legitimate or otherwise. This Phantom Menace that is the 'Silent Sentry' marks the beginning, not in this case of Star Wars, but of *Star Police*.

22 Ibid.

Chapter 3

From the Gulf War to the war in Kosovo, recent conflicts will merely have been arms fairs for American military equipment, new ways of promoting weapons and disastrously re-stimulating the military–industrial complex. In our fascination with the event of the break with the UN, we have not even noticed the beginnings of a second break – this time with NATO.

Though control of Operation 'Allied Force' in the Balkans officially lay with Javier Solana, the Secretary-General of NATO, it was the Atlantic Council (a permanent political organ of the Alliance) and its military committee which were in charge of the war directives so far as the engagement of forces in Kosovo was concerned. But all this too was merely pretence, since, from the second phase of this air war onwards, the management of the conflict was in the hands of an 'informal directorate', consisting of the United States and its privileged allies – Britain, France and Germany – to the detriment of the fifteen other member nations of NATO.

This was a discreet, furtive break with the past, as befits a period of 'information war', but it was a significant, violent break so far as the future of war in the twenty-first century is concerned. If, in fact, shortly after the collapse of the Berlin Wall, the war in the Persian Gulf marked the end of the status quo in the *military balance* between the great blocs of East and West, the war in Kosovo marks, for its part, the end of the status quo in the *political balance* between the nations. Hence, with the sudden relaunch of the arms race, it ushers in the pursuit of a second deterrence, capable of re-establishing, if not stability in the age of the 'single market', then at least American leadership.

Zbigniew Brzezinski wrote on this matter that it was no exaggeration to state that the failure of NATO would mean both 'the end of the credibility of the Atlantic Alliance and the weakening of American world leadership'. The consequences, he argued, 'would be devastating for planetary stability'.[23] Our expert, a former

23 Z. Brzezinski, 'Guerre totale contre Milosevic', *Le Monde*, 17 April 1999.

national security adviser to President Jimmy Carter, is apparently worried here about the unbalance in the Atlantic Alliance, without realizing that the decline of *coalition warfare* on the part of NATO, and also the programmed end of *coalition politics* on the part of the UN, can make a very substantial contribution to creating total American supremacy. This may enable the USA to impose, in the future, another type of 'global strategic concept' which is infinitely more ambitious than the vague, nebulous conception enunciated in Washington on 23 April 1999 on the fiftieth anniversary of NATO.

This is a **globalitarian** concept, untrammelled either by concern for NATO or for the UN, inasmuch as its fields of competence and intervention might be said to be not so much *geophysical* as *meta-geophysical* – the 'temporal' dimension of the strategic supremacy of the USA here winning out once and for all over the 'spatial' dimensions of the old geo-strategic supremacy of the Atlantic Alliance.

Let us now take a look at a contradiction which says much about US ambitions here: on 6 April, President Clinton declared: 'I want to say again, the United States would never choose force as anything other than a last option.'[24] Yet, shortly before the Washington summit,

24 'Remarks by the President at Hate Crimes Announcement', The White House, Office of the Press Secretary, 6 April 1999 (10:51 a.m. EDT).

we learned that Germany and Canada had been unable to get NATO's nuclear strategy revised, *the United States having refused to abandon recourse to nuclear weapons*. And when we are told of the need to open up the Atlantic Alliance to new members and new countries on the fringes of the European continent, this is couched in terms of the American resolve to promote an extensive conception of NATO's geographical responsibilities *which would lead, in the end, to making any unanimous decision-making process slower and slower*, thus indirectly reinforcing the leadership of the United States in the areas of orbital and cybernetic warfare.

Let us turn, for a moment, to the French defence minister, Alain Richard. 'We are not enchanted with NATO,' he says, 'but it is the only tool which exists that allows us to pool military resources in real time.' When you understand the nature of the 'silence procedure' (in which silence on a decision signifies consent) imposed by the NATO military general staff in Brussels in order to carry out the air strikes on Yugoslavia, you can see what kind of political impasse would result from extending such 'coalition warfare' to ever greater numbers of increasingly scattered countries. Let us note, moreover, by way of confirmation, that General Wesley Clark is constantly complaining to the US Congress of the obstacles the NATO allies put in his way, and venting his frustration at having to deal with a number of recalcitrant nations capable of imposing a veto on some of his strategic objectives. We may rest assured, then, that NATO's fiasco in the Balkans will be attributed to the ditherings of the allies of the American force and not in any way to the incompetence of its Commander-in-Chief.

And this will be so even though the strategy of air strikes is an American decision, which all the other parties contest, including the British – John Chipman of the International Institute of Strategic Studies declaring in late April that the strategy adopted in the Balkans campaign and its application raised serious questions about NATO's capacity to conceive and execute complex military operations.

One cannot but be worried, in Europe, by this disastrous incompetence on the part of the Atlantic Alliance to carry on a coalition war. As indeed is General Sir Michael Rose, the former UN Commander-in-Chief in Bosnia, when he argues that NATO's strategy has failed because the use of air raids alone is a totally unsuitable way to achieve the declared objectives and contends that 'NATO cannot continue to ignore the fact that it has suffered a strategic defeat'.[25] By way of conclusion to this catalogue of disillusionment, let us also cite General

---

25 General Sir Michael Rose, 'Nato must head for a door marked exit', *The Times*, 18 April 1999.

Naumann, Chairman of the Military Committee of the Atlantic Alliance, who declared in his farewell speech of 5 April: 'We have to find a way to reconcile the conditions of a coalition war with the principles of a military operation, such as surprise or the use of irresistible force. We didn't use either in Yugoslavia.' Continuing this assessment of the shortcomings of the operation, the first German general to be engaged in conflict since 1945 went on to deplore the fact that 'this NATO air campaign is clearly being conducted by the United States.' In conclusion, he added, 'The gulf between Europe and the United States goes on widening . . . We urgently need European countries to make a greater effort in the area of defence.'[26]

It is evident, then, that even if the North Atlantic Treaty Organization stole a march on the United Nations in this disastrous Balkans campaign, its inability to conduct a coalition war in Kosovo leads, ultimately, to the failure of post-Cold War geopolitics. Above all, however, it leads to a crisis of the sovereignty of the nation state.

Apart from the extension of the Alliance's geographical area of influence and the swelling of its competences,

26 'Un général de l'OTAN déplore les contraintes', *Le Monde*, 6 May 1999.

the strategic concept proposed in Washington at the fiftieth anniversary of NATO presented a disparate range of threats to peace, ranging from civil criminality to drugs, from terrorism to weapons of mass destruction. The Europeans, troubled by what they perceived to be an over-ambitious shopping-list of aims, decided to confine themselves to the creation of an 'office' to co-ordinate the exchange of information in the battle against the proliferation of weapons of mass destruction.

But it would be to understand nothing of the Pentagon's **revolution in military affairs** if we were to confine ourselves merely to the *comprehensive insurance* aspect without grasping the hegemonic dimension of the American armed forces at this millennium end. With this new revolution of the military–industrial complex, the Pentagon is preparing to invest several billions of dollars over the next five years, part of it, admittedly, in new weapons development, but the major part in the cybernetic monitoring and surveillance systems necessitated by the implementation of 'information warfare'.[27] In its Annual Report for 1999, the US Department of Defense stated that such expenditure is 'essential to ensuring that tomorrow's forces continue to dominate across the full spectrum of military

27 See Paul Virilio, *The Information Bomb*, Verso, London, 2000.

operations'.[28] Such an ambition to ensure supremacy on all fronts indefinitely can only indicate a degree of immoderation and mania exceeding that of the military forces of yesteryear.

Given this **globalitarian** aspect of American power, which is a product of the instantaneous globalization of geopolitical relations and, above all, of *the geophysical finitude of the planet on which we live*, we can better understand the importance of US aero-spatial operations over Europe and the Near East and, even better, that country's resolve – with the recent decision by President Clinton to begin research and development into a National Missile Defence (NMD) system – to guarantee its supremacy with regard to *the control of circumterrestrial space.*

Lieutenant-Colonel Randy Weidenheimer of the US Air Force, who is engaged in that research, recently argued that the US had so far regarded space as the theatre of military challenges only with regard to communications, reconnaissance and surveillance. Now, he explained, they had *to be able to use their satellites as genuine weapons.*

Not only is such a statement fraught with serious

28 Annual Defense Report 1999, chapter 1. Cited in Michael T. Klare, 'US aims to win on all fronts', *Le Monde diplomatique* (English language edition), May 1999.

consequences, since it overrides the political decision not to militarize circumterrestrial space, but there is a danger that it will bring with it unilateral renunciation by the United States of the Anti-Ballistic Missiles Treaty of 1972, and also throw into doubt the Strategic Arms Reduction agreements. Lastly, when the United States proposes a strategic axis between Japan and America, which would lead in the long run to Japanese participation in a Missile Defence programme extended to Asia, it is not difficult to see the implications of this for Beijing. And all at the very moment when the Chinese embassy has been destroyed *by accident* using *bombs with satellite guidance systems*!

After dragging the old USSR into the race to the death of President Reagan's famous 'Star Wars', President Clinton's United States, undoubtedly believing it won the Cold War thanks to the industrial feats of **Pentagon capitalism** – enmeshing the Eastern bloc enemy in unproductive military expenditure – now seems to want to drag the United Nations (and also its NATO partners) down this same deadly path. It seems to want to do so by re-launching a race for arms supremacy, the declared aim of which would be to wear down one by one the economies which currently compete with the great Wall Street market.

Defensive, offensive . . . To refer to NATO as a transatlantic defensive structure, is to lose sight of the importance of logistics in the organization of industrial and post-industrial warfare. Since the appearance of the atom bomb, logistics has been far more important than good old strategy, since nuclear deterrence can be maintained only by constant innovation in weapons systems capable of surprising and hence defeating the enemy – or, to put it more precisely, defeating the 'opponent/ partner' in this *total economic war*. At this twentieth century's end, *strategic offensive* no longer so much means invasion – the impure war of mass extermination of civilian populations – as the permanent development of a **global arsenal** which can deter the opponent/partner in this war game. The conduct of war, kept pure of any effectuation on the ground, now achieves success through the invention of new weapons: atmospheric and extra-atmospheric armaments, such as aircraft, missiles or military satellites – with the laser weapons of 'anti-satellite' satellites waiting in the wings.

Behind the apparent absurdity of the strategy of air strikes on Yugoslavia lies concealed, then, a mutation in post-industrial armaments and in what we used to call the 'arsenal of the free world'. After the IMF or the WTO, and beyond NATO and the United Nations, preparations are being made for the emergence of a **world security force**, which would depend not so much on a UN coalition policy as on the pure deterrent power of a 'weapons ecosystem' closely combining the **atom** and **information** bombs. This would be achieved by developing a new type of deterrence, in which the *defensive* aspect of the old coalitions of the NATO type was replaced once and for all by the *deterrent* (in other words, purely *offensive*) aspect of a global power which the United States has hankered after ever since the explosion in the New Mexican desert and their win, on a technical knock-out, over the Empire of the Rising Sun.

Back to square one. The last war of the twentieth century is like the first: an industrial war dragging Europe and the world into a race to the death, with Auschwitz and Hiroshima – after Verdun – as its tragic symbols.

Let us recall, lastly, a forgotten fact, or rather one that has been lost sight of: *deterrence is not divisible.* The recognition of this fact prompted General de Gaulle's ostentatious withdrawal from NATO, and his decision to launch the project whereby France developed its own '*force de frappe*'. What the *last great power* is now actively seeking is identical in its solitary and hegemonic dimension: hence its exceeding the scope of the UN today and of NATO tomorrow. To the point that the fiasco currently afflicting the Atlantic Organization cannot but hasten the establishment of a **second deterrence** – both cybernetic and aero-spatial – which will render the political status quo of the United Nations definitively obsolete.

'The accident reveals the substance', wrote Aristotle in his wisdom. Taking this as our guide, the 'collateral damage' and other military 'mishaps' affecting Serbia – and also neighbouring countries – such as the landing of five Cruise Missiles on a suburb of Sofia and, most importantly, the 'accidental' destruction of the Chinese embassy in Belgrade – cannot but considerably reinforce the sense of *technical chaos* in this NATO campaign.

Having gone from the extremism of total war in the early years of the century to the extremism of nuclear deterrence in the middle of that same century, only one step remained before we arrived, on the eve of the twenty-first century, at the militarily *revolutionary* and politically *reactionary* concept of **total deterrence**, both nuclear and societal, definitively transcending the sovereignty of nations. This is no longer a *geo-strategic* concept, as was the concept of a balance of terror between East and West, but an *eco-strategic*, monopolistic concept of **global** deterrence, based not so much on a threat from weapons of mass destruction as on the threat that a *full-scale accident* may befall the cybernetic and energy ecosystem which now regulates the vitality of post-industrial societies – such as those bombs which are capable of cutting off a nation's electricity or the viruses or bugs (e.g. Y2K) capable of bringing about veritable **cyber-Chernobyls**.

So, from the **absolute**, thermonuclear weapon, capable of extinguishing all life on the planet, to the absolute deterrence of an **atomic** and **informatic** weapons ecosystem capable of totally paralysing the life of societies, it has been but a small step. A small step for twentieth-century man, but one giant leap for the next century's inhumanity . . .

'I have been everything and everything is nothing,' observed the Stoic emperor Marcus Aurelius. The dominion of globalization is precisely this: when the logic of power becomes absolute, it wins out over the – political – logic of civil peace and the rule of law and nudges open the Pandora's box of social implosion. The old Soviet Union was the first to test out this proposition; others will follow.

Here, the *geographical metastasis* of the Alliance of the nineteen European nations, soon to be joined by others, indicates the pathological swelling of NATO. If the North Atlantic Treaty Organization is indeed intent on becoming the biggest show in town, it will turn into the United Nations Organization. But, conversely, if in the future the UN – in the name of the new duty to intervene – equips itself with a *force of military coercion* equal to its humanitarian ambitions, it will soon develop the same delusions as NATO. This convergence might be said to be the inevitable, unremarked consequence of a political economy which still refuses to face up to the 'ecosystemic' character of the *temporal compression* which has befallen it in the era of the cybernetic globalization of nations.

If the watchword of the monarchical power of bygone centuries was 'divide and rule', the arrogance of power manifests itself today not only through *local division*, but much rather through *global multiplication:* the growing confusion of nation states at the acceleration of economico-political procedures, the interactive feedback between the **global** and the **local**. Significantly, in the era of the 'information revolution', the same process is now affecting **disinformation**: whereas in the past it was lack of information and censorship which characterized the denial of democracy by the totalitarian state, the opposite is now the case. Disinformation is achieved by flooding TV viewers with information, with apparently contradictory data. The truth of the facts is censured by **over-information**, as we have seen from the press and television discussing the Balkans. The globalitarian state, built out of economico-strategic alliances, is no longer old 'Anastasia' with her scissors: it is **Babel**. Now **more is less**. And in some cases, less than nothing. Deliberate manipulation and unintentional accidents have become indistinguishable.[29]

Hence the sense of 'de-realization' which afflicts people and, in the end, prevents public opinion from being fully signed up and committed to NATO's

29 See P. Virilio, *The Information Bomb*, op. cit.

surrealistic war against Serbia: '"Everything has grown irrational these last few days", said a Belgrade student, an opponent of the Milosevic regime, "It's impossible to be correctly informed, either by listening to the Serb media, picking up the Western media or surfing the Internet. Wherever you turn, there's just propaganda."'[30] Information warfare is precisely this. It is not just the guidance of missiles using 'electronic warfare' techniques, but the remote guidance of confusion. It is this chaos of opinion which complements, which puts the finishing touch to, the chaos of destruction on the ground.

This state of affairs, in which incomprehension and ignorance of the truth are at their height, radically undermines the classical psychological doctrines – and even the old Clausewitzian theories – of warfare. This is an 'aero-orbital' war, which has to pay political heed now to the roundness of the terrestrial globe, and also to the temporal compression of the data used to conduct the fighting.

These military systems, the communications weapons, which are the non-lethal – or, if one prefers, the **pure – weapons** of this new human rights war, have a long

30 Danilo, 'Milosevic c'est une chose, la Serbie une autre', *L'Humanité hebdo*, 16 May 1999.

history which goes back to the conflict in Vietnam and, most importantly, to the end of the Cold War in Europe. In the period of controversy around the deployment of Cruise Missiles in Europe in the 1980s, linked to the deployment by the Soviets of the notorious SS 20s in East Germany, the Americans had modified their European strategy with the adoption of the concept of so-called **'first strikes'** against the enemy's rear. In the face of the danger of the 40,000 tanks of the Red Army's armoured divisions sweeping across Europe, the Pentagon had decided to attack the enemy's logistics and its rearward bases with pre-emptive nuclear strikes on Soviet territory itself. For want of an officially **offensive** strategic concept, forbidden by the doctrine of deterrence, the United States and NATO, faced with the forces of the Warsaw Pact, had developed the idea of an aerial **right of pre-emption** on enemy territory – given that there was no possibility of competing with the Soviet armoured divisions and reacting to their assault at the terrestrial level by a counter-attack in Eastern Europe.

In view of the clear disequilibrium between NATO and Warsaw Pact ground forces, the aerial route was the only way out. Hence the development of Cruise Missiles and Drones, over-flying Eastern Europe at low altitude to strike at the heart of the enemy's supply lines. This type of **automatic** intervention with no danger of human losses – *a new form of the 'gunboat diplomacy'* so dear to maritime, colonial powers – was to prove the form best suited, after the fall of the Berlin Wall, to the security aims of that future 'world policeman', the United States.

In the early 1990s, the Tomahawks aimed at Leningrad and Moscow simply had to be reprogrammed and directed towards Baghdad or Basra. We know what followed, with the launch in 1998 of Cruise Missiles on Khartoum and Afghanistan. Tomahawk Cruise Missiles, which, alongside Patriot Missiles, were the weapon of choice in the Gulf War, ushered in the deregulation of nuclear deterrence, **pre-emptive** strikes (conventional or otherwise) becoming the new name for the post-Clausewitzian **offensive**, succeeding the 'gunboat politics' which had filled that role for the Western sea powers up to the beginning of the twentieth century. The Anglo-Saxon powers, which subscribe to the old naval theory of 'the fleet in being', have just surreptitiously extended to aero-naval and aero-terrestrial space the logic of force which consisted in being able to surprise the enemy without taking on the whole of his forces and without declaring war . . . *without, in fact, coming into contact at all!*

After the *ground offensive*, the invasion of countries along a now obsolete 'front line', we have today the *aero-orbital offensive*.[31] After the gunboat politics of

31 P. Brunet, 'La défense laser anti-missiles en examen', *Air et Cosmos*, 21 May 1999.

Commodore Perry, forcing Japan to open up to international trade in 1853, we have today Cruise Missile politics, with the continuity of the open sky winning out over the contiguity of land borders. One can understand why the China of the Celestial Empire and Japan, a former victim of this kind of **intrusive** politics, are troubled today by this sudden resurgence of the Western ambition to rule, if not over 'international law', then at least over the space-time of their national sovereignty.

The other aspect of the 'revolution in military affairs' very clearly concerns **non-lethal weapons**, the purpose of which is not so much to destroy the enemy as to neutralize him. From this apparently 'humanitarian' perspective, the graphite bombings of May, which consisted in *switching off Serbia's electricity system without destroying its basic infrastructure*, are similar to the ecological effects of the neutron bomb – an atomic bomb designed to exterminate enemy combatants without destroying their installations or contaminating their environment in the long term. In both cases, what one is seeking to eliminate is only ever life, the opponent's energetic vitality.

But let us leave aside this aspect of the post-modern arsenal for the time being. Since the conflict in Vietnam the United States has, with the assistance of several Nobel prize winners for physics, been deploying weapons *on the electronic battlefield*, the avowed aim of which is no longer destruction pure and simple, but rather the secondary effects of the transformation of the combat environment and the modification of the combatants' personalities: dioxin defoliants, such as Agent Orange; cluster bombs capable of creating sudden clearings in the vegetation where assault helicopters could be landed more easily; chemical incapacitants with a power to disturb the soldier's state of mind, etc.

With its progress blocked by the increasingly extreme nature of the atom bomb and its destructive capacities, which had become thermonuclear, American logistics set about research and development on a new type of arsenal in which *the precipitation of accidents of all kinds* was soon to take precedence over destroying or killing people by exploding molecular or nuclear devices. This was a particularly disconcerting aspect of the military-industrial complex, but an aspect which was, nonetheless, contemporaneous with the Anglo-Saxon school of ecological thought. *War pure* of any 'apocalyptic' effectuation, as represented at that time by East–West deterrence and its arms race, led to the search for *pure weapons,* capable, if not of ensuring victory without bloodshed, at least of reducing the symbolic/media impact of the blood – the blood of soldiers, essentially. A *clean war*, which went beyond the principle of the *just war* of the old free-world fighters.

Lastly, we would not be in a position to understand the unleashing of this entirely new 'human rights' war in the Balkans if we did not grasp this initial blurring of the 'military' and the 'humanitarian' – a confusion which began not, as is often claimed, after the war against Iraq, nor even with the disastrous American intervention in Somalia, but more than thirty years ago in Vietnam with the post-modern mutation of *the arsenal of total war.*

When, speaking of collateral damage in Kosovo, James Shea, the NATO spokesperson, declared 'No conflict in human history has ever been accident-free,'[32] he had, without knowing it, hit the nail on the head! With the Pentagon's revolution in military affairs, the *jackpot of accidents* will 'roll over' week on week and will generate the utmost confusion between the official declaration of objectives (whether or not these are achieved) and the semi-official, discreet determination to cause *systemic accidents* and other 'chain reactions' in the enemy. Here, the model of viral contamination and (atomic or cybernetic) irradiation clearly shows itself: the aim is no longer so much to *blow up* a structure as to *neutralize* the enemy's *infrastructure* by spreading *breakdown and panic* in his ranks and all around him by the sudden interruption of all coherent, co-ordinated activity.

It would seem, in fact, to be less a question of

---

32 NATO briefing, 15 April 1999.

pursuing victory or peace as of the United States relentlessly pursuing the passivity both of its opponents and its competitors. Thus, the conquest of **panoptical** ubiquity would lead to the conquest of **passivity**, with populations not so much going down to military defeat, as in the past, but succumbing to mental confusion. Where once the defeated were reduced to slavery, now their public opinion is simply thrown into disarray by technical chaos. It is surely clear, here again, that information warfare is the beneficiary in this subtle development of battlefield disorganization.

With its logic bombs, computer viruses and year 2000 (Y2K) bugs and other forms of system deregulation – such as the disturbance of the Global Positioning System in the summer of 1999 – NATO's just and clean (or almost clean) war in the Balkans marvellously illustrates the coming *militarization of the accident* and, after the search for the *local accident* through use of the combat gases or dirty bombs of the twentieth century, the desperate search for that *global accident* which will be capable, in the twenty-first century, of destabilizing the daily life of nations and their economies by the sudden interruption of their energy systems – and doing so in the clear absence of any *declaration of war.*

With the **information** bomb now complementing the apocalyptic threat of the atom bomb with a strictly *cybernetic* danger of its own, we can better guess at the use to be made of the hackers and other computer buccaneers recently engaged by Pentagon capitalism, and the apparent or simulated concern of the US Defense Department at the possibility of an **electronic Pearl Harbor**, with future conflicts ending not so much in defeat or victory for one of the protagonists, as in chaos – *the transpolitical chaos of nations.*

After the explosion in the New Mexican desert and, most importantly, those at Hiroshima and Nagasaki, came a blessed period for the USA when *atomic deterrence was not shared* – not even with a sort of adversary/partner, as was later to be the case with the Soviet Union. **The first deterrence**. Then came a gradual degeneration of this *absolute deterrence* with the balance of terror between East and West, which was termed deterrence of the **strong** by the **strong**. Even later, this maximalist theory of Mutually Assured Destruction (MAD) came up against the equalizing power of the atom and deterrence of the **strong** by the **weak**, the historical example of which is General de Gaulle's *force de frappe*, an example of the identification of state sovereignty with the possession of atomic weapons.

Lastly, with the era of the proliferation of nuclear weapons, the theory of the deterrence of the **mad** by the **strong**, underscored by the persistent conflict with Iraq, has opened the Pandora's box of military delusion, though, after the nuclear tests by India and

Pakistan – countries currently at war in Kashmir – the very last theory in this series has not eventuated: the deterrence of the **weak** by the **weak**. Unless . . . Unless we take the view that, beyond this threshold, the equalizing power of the atom should disappear and give way to an absurd theory: the deterrence of the **mad** by the **mad**!

Given this long 'geo-strategic' decadence of contemporary history, which by its very instability greatly threatens the peace, the recent resolve to override the sovereignty of nations with the famous '*humanitarian duty to intervene*' further adds to the chaos, to the threat of the geopolitical destabilization of the world.

In this sense, NATO's first war in Eastern Europe augurs badly for the United States' capacity to ensure a lasting peace in the era of the global proliferation of the dangers to which we have just briefly referred. For want of being able to *abolish the bomb*, we have decided, then, to *abolish the state*, a nation state which is now charged with all 'sovereignist' vices and all 'nationalist' crimes, thereby exonerating a military–industrial and scientific complex which has spent a whole century innovating in horror and accumulating the most terrifying weapons – from asphyxiating gases and bacteriological weapons to the thermonuclear device, not to mention the future ravages of the information bomb or of a genetic bomb that will be capable not merely of abolishing the nation state, but the people, the population, by the 'genomic' modification of the human race.

It will come as no surprise, then, if we conclude that, whatever the political outcome of the Balkan *après-guerre*, this conflict marks the turn of the millennium. By re-starting once and for all the *race for arms supremacy* (in atomic and aero-space weaponry) – in other words, the *race to exhaust the nations economically* – the first NATO war has, in the name of human rights, ushered in the 'unbalance of terror' between East and West.

In the face of this relentless, blinkered flight forward – which is, above all, a flight to altitude – the United States is aiming to attain the blessed state of a **second deterrence**, a deterrence without an adversary or partner; hence the low degree of importance the State Department and the Pentagon quickly accorded the Kosovo fiasco – a NATO fiasco, which reinforced the resolve of the last great power to ensure a flawless hegemony in the twenty-first century over economic and political globalization, to the detriment of a coalition warfare which has clearly revealed its limitations, just like the old peaceful *coalition politics* advocated by the UN.

On 14 April 1999, less than a month before the end of the Balkans conflict, President Clinton's adviser for Europe, Ivo Daalder, declared that NATO had failed lamentably in not achieving its minimum objective in

Kosovo. What is patent at any rate, ten years after the fall of the Berlin Wall, is the inability of the European Community to provide any kind of political sovereignty in defence terms for a continent which has, in the twentieth century, undergone what can justly be described as a *hundred years war.*

Chapter 4

Nothing is still a programme,
Even nihilism is a dogma

(Cioran)

In June 1999, the United Nations Food and Agriculture Organization (FAO) reported that thirty countries – sixteen of them in Africa – were suffering serious food shortages. One of the countries on that list was . . . Yugoslavia. *The desert is spreading*, they say. Yet it is not the desert that is spreading over the planet, but the *urban wasteland* – that place where, without ever mixing, the multitude of ethnic microcosms survive – in the shanty towns, the half-way hostels, the sink estates . . .

Recently, when some young North Africans were asked why they did not want to stay in the Maghreb and preferred to emigrate, they replied, with the simplicity that comes of stating the obvious: '*Because there's nothing here to take!*' They could just as well have said, '*Because it already looks like a desert here!*' The 'deportees' in the 'camps' of our urban wastelands are not, as our ministers go on joyfully repeating, 'savages' or even 'new barbarians'. In reality, they are merely indicating the irresistible emergence of a previously almost unknown level of deprivation and human misery. They are waste-products of a military–industrial, scientific civilization which has applied itself for almost two centuries to depriving individuals of the knowledge and skill accumulated over generations and millennia, before a post-industrial upsurge occurred which now seeks to reject them, on the grounds of definitive uselessness, to *zones of lawlessness* where they are exposed defenceless to the exactions of *kapos* of a new kind.

It is no use, then, speculating on the regional aspects of the Yugoslav conflict when you understand that it is not the **world-city**, but the great **world urban wasteland** which now extends to the eastern portals of Europe. The great urban wasteland, with its bands of predators – such as the UCK or the Serbian irregulars – whose methods and excesses (kidnapping, extortion, torture, murder, arms and drug trafficking) shade dangerously into those of the mafia families and other 'honourable societies' of Europe, America and Asia.

Indeed, the Allies have learned to their cost in their offensive against the Serbs that the paramilitary groups they had armed were not very interested in *making war*. Indeed, they preferred to *thumb their noses at war, never coming together at any particular point.*[33] On the other hand, as soon as the Albanian refugees began to get back to Kosovo at the end of June, it was clear that the 'open frontier' enabled the leaders and bosses of the mafias from the Kukes and Tropoje regions to gain a foothold in the country. 'There are more and more big cars about on the roads, with tinted windows and Albanian number plates or no number plates at all,' writes a correspondent. 'Two days ago, these men of the shadows and the shady deals reached Mitrovica and Pristina, having first established a base in the Pecs region.'[34]

The fluidity of this criminal osmosis largely explains the spread of chaos and ruin in Latin America and Africa where, as Jimmy Carter observed, crossing the continent the traveller is constantly passing through countries that are prey to conflicts which are of interest to no one. And, we might add, to conflicts *which never end*. Balkanization, Sicilianization, endo-colonization are

33 On the dangers of 'people's wars', see Clausewitz, *On War*, Princeton University Press, Princeton, NJ, 1976.

34 *Le Journal du Dimanche*, 27 June 1999.

merely the outdated words for this permanent warfare, which is no longer *civil* war, but war *waged against civilians* – this perpetual menace which, sooner or later, causes the emigration, in panic, of (pillaged, ransomed and raped) local populations towards the last lands of Cockaigne where *the rule of law* still exists. This tragic curbing of *popular rights*, which signals the fundamental reversal that is currently occurring on a ruined planet, where *there will soon be nothing left to take*. We need be in no doubt that, more than ever in the twenty-first century, the abandonment of the old *anthropocentrism* will be on the agenda. With the appearance of new forms of bio-political conditioning, in which the *other* will no longer be considered as an *alter ego*, nor even as a potential enemy (with whom reconciliation is always possible), but as the ultimate quarry. Nietzsche had, in his day, predicted the imminent arrival of this new misanthropy – *an anthropophagy which would have no particular ritual*, as he put it. Unless . . . unless the revolutionary innovations of the biotechnologies, by abolishing the last taboos of a degenerate humanism, have not already taken us, without our knowing it, into this new biocracy.

A new aspect which has emerged – ten years after the ideological collapse of the Soviet Union – and which reveals this imminent mutation, is the breakdown we have seen in the Balkans of the *moral front* which previously claimed to justify Western military interventions in the name of the 'defence of the values of the free world'.[35] The discreet abandonment of the old 1940s 'programmes for world peace' explains why being spokesperson for – or, even worse, commentator on – the parade of American technology in the Balkans, was the most hazardous job in the NATO hierarchy:

> In forty days of conflict, three high-ranking officers have already fallen in the information war. None was up to the job: with their confused comments, contradictory explanations and flagrant untruths, they had to be dropped for lack of credibility . . . It is to be hoped that the next one to go over the top in the media war will last out for more than a week.[36]

As a TV reporter on the French channel TF1 was to say, '*They don't know how to handle this business at all.*'

If the *phoney war* in Kosovo was not to become a *dirty war* in the eyes of international opinion, it was

35 On 6 January 1941, President Roosevelt delivered his famous State of the Union message on the 'Four Freedoms'. From being initially a blueprint for a social system, that text became a war aim, being subsequently embodied in the Atlantic Charter of 14 August 1941.

36 *Le Figaro*, 7 May 1999.

urgent, as Pierre-Luc Séguillon observed on 28 May on LCI,[37] that

> Slobodan Milosevic should at last be charged by the International Criminal Tribunal for the former Yugoslavia so as to legitimate the Allies' campaign and a war unleashed by NATO in violation, not only of the UN Charter, but also of the Charter of the Atlantic Alliance – the former authorizing recourse to armed action only to enforce a decision of the Security Council, the latter stipulating that the Alliance is a defensive organization and that its members are committed to settling any dispute in which they might be involved by peaceful means.

In fact, nothing of these ideal dispositions remained when, on 2 June, shortly after Milosevic was charged by prosecutor Louise Arbour, the International Court of Justice at the Hague declared inadmissible the action brought by Serbia requesting a halt to the Allied bombing.[38] This rejection on the part of the oldest court of law

37 La Chaîne de l'Information. [Trans.]

38 On Thursday 10 June, the very day hostilities ended in Yugoslavia, prosecutor Louise Arbour resigned from the International Criminal Tribunal to take up an important post in the legal hierarchy of her country. This Canadian law

of the United Nations received virtually no coverage in the Western media.

Extraordinarily, the 'justice of nations' discreetly retreated behind the International Criminal Tribunal for the Former Yugoslavia (ICTY), that makeshift judicial structure, which was called upon to provide an illegal war with a hasty legitimacy, but which had every need to legitimate its own existence, as indeed was underscored by Jean-Jacques Heintz on 7 June 1999 during a conference organized by the Nantes law faculty. This French law officer, clerk to the ICTY, declared in effect that the body was a 'judicial laboratory' *which, in order to justify its existence*, had at first tried to pick up 'a few little cases' and was not, indeed, empowered to call suspects before it.

Yet, on that very day, we learned that two Bosnian Serbs, charged by this 'court of experimental justice', had been arrested by British KFOR soldiers at Prijedor in the north-west of Bosnia. This raised to 31 (out of 66) the number of those charged with 'minor offences' who had fallen into the hands of a police that was both military and anational, as NATO confirmed on 18 June when it issued a mandate to the forces deployed in

officer is the first to have laid charges against a serving foreign head of state.

Kosovo to assist the ICTY's investigators . . . while awaiting the expected arrival of the FBI.

States of emergency, special tribunals – between the countless exactions of the one side and the 'judicial laboratories' of the other, one wonders, with Jack London's Mr Owen, whether, in the near future, there will still be '*such a thing as civil law*' on the planet.[39] As for that 'floating sea of opinions' on which the new international legislation is doing its best to chart a course, the question arises why one type of aggression (the primitive type – Milosevic's) is judged criminal by the ICTY, whereas another (the high-tech type – NATO's) was not even worthy of consideration by an international court of law like that at the Hague? Is this because, since the conflict in the Persian Gulf, American forces have boasted endlessly of the 'surgical precision' of their strikes? One might, as a consequence, suppose that a just war would be one characterized by justness of aim, the high technological level of an attack becoming the warrant of its morality and legality . . . Yet, since the middle of the Serbian affair, NATO lost this presumption of high-tech innocence when it brutally intensified its bombing, thus revealing its desire to do lasting harm to

39 Jack London, *The Iron Heel* (chapter 8: 'The Machine Breakers').

all the civilian populations of the region by the systematic destruction of their habitat.

As a result, opinion began to turn against the Allies, everyone coming to ask late in the day whether this humanitarian war and its high-tech arsenal did not in reality form a kind of Jekyll and Hyde pairing. If we held to the high-tech credo of the good doctor Jekyll, every method of spreading violence to inflict maximum pain on civilian populations should have been excluded as a matter of course from this conflict – such as those *long-term indirect strategies* with which, unfortunately, Mr Hyde is only too familiar, involving the application of economic blockades (Cuba, Libya, Iraq, etc.), which create social, sanitary and institutional paralysis . . . or the support given to powerfully armed paramilitary groups (Joseph Kennedy's Katangans, the Khmer Rouge, the Taliban, the UCK), promoting the spread of the lawless no-go areas of the world's urban wastelands. We can see, then, that all the current legal cavilling is merely a smokescreen – disinformation on an industrial scale – aimed at masking the breakdown of the apparent *equity* which, until the Kosovo affair, seemed to prevail between the great democratic nations. Lawyers *sans frontières*, judges *sans frontières*, an attempt to create an ICT (International Criminal Tribunal) at the Hague, a pale imitation of the ICTs for Yugoslavia and Rwanda, in which three of the world's major nations, two of them permanent members of the

Security Council (the USA and China) refuse to participate.

The old international relations will not survive the disappearance of this *impartiality* – this moral justice independent of law – which claimed to undergird the armed actions jointly decided by the allies of the old UN Security Council.

When the edifice of the law *ceases to be a safeguard and becomes a threat,* it is difficult to believe in the discrediting, blatant though it is, of courts which are the legacy of an already long-standing established order. In the Balkans, it was no longer a question of instituting a *just war*, but a *legitimate* or even a legalist war – a war tailored to the interests of the world's last superpower and its absolute supremacy, particularly in the fields of satellite surveillance and information-gathering.

As in the old, statolatrous days of the ancient Romans – whom the Americans have always fervently admired – any activity, head of state or leader seen as threatening by this new unilateral legalism is now to be pursued, deposed, destroyed and punished for the crime of anti-Americanism. McCarthyism in the fifties gave us an idea of this legalism, before the many bombardments carried out without a mandate in Iraq and elsewhere brought it into even clearer focus. A Livy-style legalism, a new cadastral law, exercized from space by the United States, on the lines of the old centuriation: 'the indelible mark of a seizure of the Earth, where a division is made in order to dominate, this being the basis of the education of the masses.'[40] 'Tremble and obey!' The end of the balance of nuclear terror and the new world supremacy of the United States required the restructuring of the old front of fear.

So, after the fall of the Berlin Wall, we saw the development of a strange 'defence of the human species', popularized in the media by any number of 'TV marathons' and other interactive shows (on social, health and ecological issues). In actual fact, these were intended to prepare people's minds for future large-scale humanitarian manoeuvres of a much less peaceful kind, such as those in Kosovo. Successful manoeuvres, since, on that latter occasion, one clearly saw 'the birth of an immense upsurge of solidarity in favour of the Kosovars, sustained by stars from show-biz, the cinema and finance'.

Here the *missionary* element of the colonial massacre or the *messianic* dimension of the world wars with their mass slaughter are supplanted by the *humanitarian* impulse – overcoming even religious affiliations, since Westerners were going to the aid of Muslim populations who were in principle hostile to them. '*Faith begins with terror*' – the theologian's device is as appropriate now as

---

40 Colonel Barrader, *Fossatum Africae*, Editions Arts et métiers graphiques, Paris, 1949.

ever it was, war propaganda being, alongside the *propaganda fide* (the propagation of religious faith from which it derived), one of the oldest forms of marketing.

This is why it was so apposite, at the end of the balance of terror, to replace the shared fear of nuclear firepower – which I have termed the *nuclear faith* – with the administration of multiple intimate and quotidian terrors. Alongside an increasingly active *terrorisme ordinaire*, the public has thus been treated, during this last decade of the century, to the repellent advertising of the Benetton kind, or the lavish shows staged to combat AIDS or cancer, with the incurably disabled and the terminally ill being paraded before the cameras. '*Prevention is cure*!' Veiled threats, creeping eugenicism, secret terrors, causes of defiance, disgust and mutual hatreds. All this leading up to those high-frequency adverts depicting the misery of the unfortunate Kosovars, decidedly involuntary bearers of a subliminal message of the same order: 'See, none of us was safe. Women, children, the old, the rich, the poor – we all fled after losing everything. You have to prepare yourselves. If you're not careful, *it will be your turn tomorrow!*'

Without a doubt, the unprecedented exercise of the new right of intervention in the internal affairs of a sovereign nation would not have been accepted by public opinion were it not for this long psychological preparation, *this total cinema* born during the Cold War with the de-neutralization of the East–West media and, in March

1983, the signature by the actor-president Ronald Reagan of *National Security Decision – Directive* 75, the first draft of 'Project Democracy', calling for an increased American propaganda effort to accompany the measures of economic repression and military effort of the USA – a manna distributed mainly in *central and eastern Europe* to support the activities of minorities and free trade unions inside the nations of the Eastern bloc.

When, in April 1999, at the beginning of the Kosovo affair, Tony Blair declared that, in this conflict, the defence of the 'new values' should supplant the defence of the historical frontiers of nations, he was repeating word for word the terms of Reagan's old *Directive* 75. In May 1999, Theodoros Pangalos, the Greek minister of foreign affairs, observed of this *topological upheaval* of nations resolved upon by Washington, 'We're in the Balkans here. And if we change one of the frontiers today, nobody can say what they will be tomorrow.' Speaking from long experience, the Greek minister knew that this was not a one-off operation that had been illegally unleashed in Kosovo, but a long process of the geographical decomposition of nations in Europe and throughout the world.

To the question posed so many times during the conflict, 'What does the United States want in the Balkans?', we should today substitute this other question: 'What did NATO want in the Balkans?' A large number of

Americans who were hostile to the military action were content to believe, like former President Carter, that, if it was to retain its credibility, NATO could not change *what had already been done*! In other words, everyone was more or less aware of being *faced with a fait accompli*.

The time has come, then, it would seem, to call things by their names and to cleave strictly to the operational reality of the event: what we have witnessed in Kosovo has been *a globalist putsch*. That is to say, a seizure of power by an anational armed group (NATO), evading the political control of the democratic nations (the UN) – evading the prudence of their diplomacy and their specific jurisdictions. It then becomes easier to understand the extent to which this *purely revolutionary* state of affairs necessitated the *mass-consumption version* of the events we have had served up to us with the aim of obtaining a popular consensus. After the humanitarian stratagem, which was beginning to wear a little thin, came the judgement '*pour l'exemple*' of a serving head of state – a kind of Western-style *fatwa* affording the twofold advantage of convincing public opinion that the allied military intervention was justified and serving as a salutary warning to any head of government who might not subscribe to the mysterious *new values* dictated by the ICT.

Adherence to the military–humanitarian dimension replaced the military–liberatory, before being itself supplanted by the noble figure of the armed dispenser of justice. With providence playing its part here, it was announced during the first week in July that British KFOR troops had discovered Serb documents in Pristina proving 'the meticulous planning of ethnic cleansing by the Belgrade leaders'. To intensify the effect of this opportune discovery and give it full media value, a secret document was at the same time removed from the safe of a small library near Los Angeles where it had lain for 54 years. That document was, we are told, the original of the Nuremberg Laws, a text, signed in Hitler's hand on the eve of the Nazi rallies of 1935, in which the 'final solution' already lay encoded.

In this connection, a journalist wrote: 'Dictators have always felt the need to give a semblance of legitimacy to their darkest schemes.'[41] As if it were not essentially the role of such 'revelations' to justify NATO's putsch and the succession of internal and external *coups d'état* which the old national entities can henceforth expect to suffer.

Similarly, the Albanian tragedy retrospectively casts light on the apparently nonsensical triggering of the Clinton/Lewinsky affair, which may now appear to have been a preparation of world opinion for the new military revolution. In 1998, the obscene attacks of Kenneth Starr and the world-wide broadcasting of Clinton's confessions made the president a global laughing-stock, but above all

41 *Le Journal du Dimanche*, 4 July 1999.

it made him *the plaything of the Pentagon.* It was also necessary, then, that in 1999 this adulterous president, former draft-dodger and defender of gays, who was held in contempt by a purportedly puritanical American army, should not be put out of office. At the time when the Kosovo conflict came about, President Clinton's poll rating was lower than it had ever been before, with many of his compatriots beginning to understand that the political power he was supposed to defend had, thanks to him, not only been made a laughing-stock, but also despoiled, and that the affair in the Balkans was perhaps *the beginning of the end* for the democratic model.

'*That which precedes the event is not necessarily its cause*,' claims the wisdom of the ancients. The century which is coming to a close has most often proved the opposite and no one can really claim to be safe from military–industrial and scientific determinism and determination – safe from that race to *the absolute essence of war* which, even in his day, Clausewitz imagined – war conceived as a 'whole, which must have one final determinate object, in which all particular objects must become absorbed'.[42] A race towards a global, universal

42 *On War*, op. cit., Book V, chapter II, 'Absolute and Real War'.

state, deriving directly from the nuclear status quo, as outlined by the physicist Werner Heisenberg in *Physics and Philosophy* or, a little later, by Ernst Jünger.[43]

In this totalitarian dramaturgy, must we regard every item of information, every event as one of the 'particular objects' intended to be absorbed in this 'whole'? Eight weeks into the NATO bombing, the satellite broadcasting of Serb television (RTS) was to be interrupted, thereby effectively violating the principle of non-discrimination, which had until then been upheld by EUTELSAT, and once again flouting UN Security Council resolutions.

At the same time, an American State Department spokesperson formally denied rumours that the US was imminently to cut off Internet connections between Yugoslavia and the rest of the world. Unlike the local, conventional television service, the **World Wide Web**, promoted in a multi-million dollar campaign at the end of the Gulf War, logically has its place in the Balkan conflict.

The Internet is of military origin and has military purposes. In the field of information it plays more or less

43 Werner Heisenberg, *Physics and Philosophy*, Harper and Row, New York, 1962 (first German edition 1958); Ernst Jünger, *Der Weltstaat*, 1960.

the same role as the *jamming* of enemy broadcasts in earlier world conflicts. As Negroponte has rightly remarked, with the 'liberation of information' on the Web, what is most lacking is *meaning* or, in other words, a *context* into which Internet users could put the facts and hence distinguish **truth** from **falsehood**. On the Web, where, as everyone knows, the terrorist temptation is constant and where the depredations of hackers are committed with impunity in a strange state of legal indeterminacy, the difference between (true) information and (false) deception fades a little more each day. In entering the looking-glass worlds of television and home computers, we are in the end left in the position of Kinglake's old 'English soldiery'. As they saw it,

> insofar as the battlefield presented itself to the bare eyesight of men, it had no entirety, no length, no breadth, no depth, no size, no shape and was made up of nothing . . . In such conditions, each separate gathering . . . went on fighting its own little battle in happy and advantageous ignorance of the general state of the action; nay, even very often in ignorance of the fact that any great conflict was raging.

As Albert Camus asserted: '*When we are all guilty, that will be true democracy.*' All guilty, all volunteers in the great interactive manoeuvres of information warfare and, above all, ignorant of the fact that any great conflict is raging.

'For the first time, there is no longer any difference between domestic and foreign policy,' declared President Clinton last year. In the context of the metapolitical undertaking which is aimed at transforming the planet into a single urban wasteland, every sign of the criminal law being diverted to new, anational tasks necessarily assumes its full meaning.

Like the creation in recent years of these curious 'ethics committees' that are supposed to convince public opinion of the harmlessness of the experimental sciences which have today largely been diverted from their proper purposes. Made up haphazardly from technical and scientific experts, a few rare 'moral' personalities and, most recently, representatives of the big corporations, the recommendations of these makeshift institutions have, as we know, long been rendered ridiculous by the research institutes and major companies of the world's most industrialized (G8) countries switching over within a few years first from chemicals to pharmaceuticals, then on to biotechnologies – those same eight countries which – once again substituting themselves for the UN! – concocted the peace plan presented to Milosevic.

Similarly, when our new 'judicial laboratories' claim to legitimate their existence by reference to an ethic drawn from the great Nuremberg trials (25 November

1945 – October 1946), the comparison seems particularly inappropriate. To appreciate this, one has simply to recall that during that unprecedented trial, in which twenty-four members of the Nazi party and eight organizations from Hitler's Germany were judged by an international military tribunal, the charges related to war crimes and, most importantly, to **conspiracy against humanity**. This was a remarkably precise charge, since it indicated that, above and beyond the blatant massacres on the battlefields and the devastation of the bombed cities, crimes of a new kind had been conceived and committed in the secrecy of the deportation camps of total war – and that they were committed, let it be noted, by way of the reform of a German judicial system which was already in decay. This was *the 'terrible secret'*[44] – the secret of the 'biological' disappearance of millions of men, women and children; millions of civilians who believed they were still protected by the rule of law, being unaware that it was no longer in force.

And with it went a new 'science of man' in which not only the nominal identity of individuals was denied, but their *anthropological identity*, their belonging to 'humanity', the living body of the human being

44 The title of a work on the holocaust by the historian Walter Laqueur. [Trans.]

becoming an object of experimentation and a *raw material* in a period of extreme shortages. But was not the peaceable, bureaucratic planning of the 'final solution', which Hannah Arendt discovered during the Adolf Eichmann trial, that of the *new anthropophagy* announced sixty years earlier by Nietzsche?

On 29 June 1999, a file bearing red swastika seals went on display at the Skirball Cultural Center in Los Angeles. This was said to be the original of the Nuremberg Laws, introducing, among other things, the code of discrimination against the Jews. The document, we are told, had been recovered by General Patton in April 1945 from the coffers of a little Bavarian town near Nuremberg. During the advance of the American Third Army in Europe, the general had been a witness: *everything contained in germ in that file had become reality*. When he returned to the United States, Patton had consequently entrusted the document to friends, the Huttingtons, the owners of a small library and gallery not far from Los Angeles, recommending that they lock it up in their safe and keep it hidden there. Subsequently, the various trustees of the library complied with the general's orders and the 'terrible secret' was thus scrupulously kept for more than half a century.

At precisely the point when *experimental tribunals* were being set up with the aim of redefining new 'human rights' on the planet, the opening of this Pandora's box –

in which not even Hope remained – puts one in mind of the reactivation of a dangerous substance . . .

At a time when plans are being hatched for the 'industrialization of living matter' and a new eugenics is secretly being elaborated, this time promoting not the natural, but the artificial, selection of the human race.

And when, right in the middle of the resolution of a 'humanitarian conflict', we can already see the first fruits of the post-war period on the front pages of our newspapers,[45] with the ravings of the gurus of historical anthropophagy, announcing that, thanks to 'the open-ended character of modern natural science', biotechnology will provide us with the tools which will

> allow us to accomplish what social engineers of the past failed to do. *At that point, we will have definitively finished human history because we will have abolished human beings as such. And then a new post-human history will begin.*[46]

---

45 The newspaper in question was *Le Monde des débats,* no. 5, July–August 1999. Fukuyama's article is printed there in translation, together with 'replies' by Alain Touraine, Immanuel Wallerstein and Joseph S. Nye. [Trans.]

46 Francis Fukuyama, 'Second Thoughts. The Last Man in a Bottle', *The National Interest*, no. 56, summer 1999, p. 33. Continuing his work of ten years earlier on the 'end of history', Fukuyama, far from admitting the absurdity of his theory, is now prophesying the 'end of humanity'.

Printed in the United States
by Baker & Taylor Publisher Services